A Glut
of
Tomatoes
& Salad
Vegetables

Ann Carr

Illustrated by
Martin MacKeown

MEREHURST PRESS
— LONDON —

The Publishers wish to thank Rosemary
Wilkinson and Malcolm Saunders for their help
with this book.

First published 1988 by Merehurst Press
5 Great James Street
London WC1N 3DA

Produced by
Malcolm Saunders Publishing Ltd
26 Ornan Road, London NW3 4QB

ISBN 0 948075 88 0

Photoset in Linotype Ehrhardt
by Fakenham Photosetting Limited
Printed in Spain

CONTENTS

My loves shall growe vp as the water
Cresses, slowly, but with a deepe roote.

(1590, Lodge)

FOREWORD

A glut of salad stuffs is the very last thing the gardener planned but is a most common problem. Shops and markets are also overflowing with tomatoes, cucumbers and lettuces; though these may be in better condition and shape than those 'home grown'. The home producer also has to cope with such disappointments as bitter cucumbers, tasteless tomatoes and lettuces producing only dark green outer leaves and no tender, crisp hearts. Sometimes it seems that the salad patch is producing more problems than ingredients for exotic dishes. And the seed packet didn't say what to do with all this salad stuff when it grew and bolted out of control.

The recipes in this book will help you use your salad glut; not just in the usual manner of freezing and preserving but straight from the garden and market place to the table.

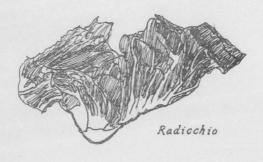

Radicchio

Breade steped in white brothe, with sodden let-tyse, or cykorie, are good to be vsed.

(1533, Elyot)

10

INTRODUCTION

The salad garden nowadays doesn't grow just the many varieties of lettuce, it also grows endives, rocket and fennel. Of these delicious salad greens one is unlikely to have a glut. It's how to use up lettuce, tomatoes, cucumbers, cress, radishes and spring onions that the gardener or glut-bargain buyer needs recipes for.

The tomato is a native of South America and strictly speaking a fruit. Although used mostly in the West as a vegetable, in the East it is used as we would use a fruit. It is the fruit of a cultivated plant belonging to the species *Lycopersicon esculentum* of the nightshade family (*Solanaceae*).

There are many varieties of tomato; many shapes and many sizes, and their colours range from rich yellow through green to a deep, dark red. There are delicious sweet little cherry tomatoes (and they really can be eaten as fresh fruit – see page 36). And there are the huge, red, salad tomatoes of southern France full of sharp flavour and tasting so good with an olive oil vinaigrette and chopped fresh basil. The tomato has contributed so much to the world's cooking. It seems to work as an emulsifier, as an acidic lift, as a salt counteracter, as a zest-giver and as a colouring agent. Tomatoes have also given

11

us tomato purée, which is added to more dishes than one could list.

In the United States and southern Europe, the tomato is grown as a major crop for use fresh, for canning, for pastes and purées, for soups, pickles, relishes and sauces. In northern Europe the tomato has to be grown with care and is generally cultivated under glass or in sheltered corners of sunny gardens and yards. The introduction

Lambs Lettuce

of 'grow bags' has meant that tomatoes can now be grown in almost any sheltered sunny corner, no matter how small.

One last bonus the tomato plant gives us is the wonderful, pungent smell of its grey-green furry leaves.

Cultivated in Egyptian times, the lettuce probably came from the East, but its origins are so ancient as to be obscure. Lettuce (*Lactuca sativa*), our common cultivated salad plant, falls into four botanical varieties,

Batavia Endive

asparagus lettuce (*asparagina*) with narrow leaves and succulent, thick stalks; cabbage lettuce (*capitata*) in two classes: butterhead and crisp-head; leaf or curly-leaved lettuce (*crispa*) and cos, a long, dark-leaved lettuce (*longifolia*). Our appreciation of the lettuce is growing and many more varieties are available in markets and stores, as well as in seed packets to grow yourself. The lovely red-leafed salad vegetables which are now

14

obtainable are, in fact, chicories or endives, as is the French 'frisée' (as its alternative names 'curly endive' or 'chicory' imply). Although easy to grow, lettuces need attention and during hot weather a lot of watering, otherwise they will be tough and bitter.

The lone, creeping plant with trailing stems and hairy leaves of the cucumber (*Cucumis sativus*) was a native of Asia, probably northern India.

Its outer skin is darkest green, while the flesh is coolest, palest green, crisp to bite into

Cabbage Lettuce

and almost as reviving as water to the palate, which is perhaps why, in the Middle East, and in hot dry climates, the cucumber is revered and served with a respect such as is generally given only to water. The tired guest may be offered first water, then a piece of cucumber. In northern Europe the cucumber, like the tomato, is generally grown under glass, and cucumber frames can still be seen in old-fashioned gardens. Grown in the open they tend to be tough and bitter, which is perhaps why they have a reputation for being windy and indigestible. In the United States they are grown as a field crop.

Cucumbers are grown in various shapes and sizes – ovoid and stumpy, a Middle Eastern salad variety; long, dark green and slender in Europe and in the United States for salads; and short, pale green and yellow, generally pickled, when it becomes known as a gherkin.

Cress, a native of Persia; rocket, a native of southern Europe; corn salad, also a native of southern Europe but growing wild in the fields, are all salad extras, added to give zest and flavour. They are unlikely to be grown in such quantities as to produce gluts. Radishes and spring onions are the root vegetables of the salad bowl and of these vegetables a small glut that might need to be used up quickly often occurs.

It is a very fine Broth which he is served up in; the
Lettice are very choyce ones.

(1671, H.M. trs. Erasmus Colloquies)

COOKS' NOTES

1. Unless specific details are given in the individual recipes, the following apply:
– spoon measurements are level
– sugar is granulated
– eggs are standard size
2. Follow either the imperial measurements or the metric but do not mix them, as they have been calculated separately.
3. As individual oven temperatures vary, use the timings in the recipes as a guide. Always preheat your oven or grill.

The
Recipes

TOMATOES

Tomatoes are now so popular they are eaten all year round and imported by the millions out of season to satisfy the huge demand. They're so delicious raw, cut in half and sprinkled with a little sugar and salt to eat at once: so wonderful, it seems a shame to cook them! But they are equally good cooked on their own as a vegetable, made into a sauce, or simply added to a soup or stew to enhance the flavour. We have become so accustomed to using the tomato to flavour and decorate dishes that we should sadly miss it if it were suddenly no longer available for use in our kitchens.

A world devoid of tomato soup, tomato sauce, tomato ketchup and tomato paste is hard to visualize.

(1984, Elizabeth David 'An Omelette and a Glass of Wine')

Tomato & Yogurt Soup

A hot or cold soup: the sweet peppers give it an unusual flavour.

Serves 4

2 tablespoons olive oil

2 lb (1 kg) ripe tomatoes, skinned and chopped

1 sweet red pepper

10 fl oz (315 ml) tomato juice

10 fl oz (315 ml) plain yogurt

1 tablespoon wine vinegar

salt and pepper, to taste

2 tablespoons chopped fresh chives

Heat oil in a saucepan, add tomatoes and stir-fry for 5–10 minutes. Purée in a blender or food processor and set aside. Grill the pepper until skin is blackened all over, then plunge in cold water and rub off skin. Chop flesh finely and set aside. Mix together tomato juice, yogurt and vinegar and process until smooth. Stir into puréed tomatoes, then add salt and pepper. Just before serving, add chopped peppers, stir well and sprinkle with chives.

Note: This soup can be made in advance but don't add sweet red peppers more than 30 minutes before serving. The peppers may be prepared in advance and kept, covered, in the fridge. If serving hot, reheat gently and do not boil.

Tomato & Orange Soup

A creamy soup, good served hot or cold.

Serves 4–6
1 tablespoon cooking oil
1 onion, chopped
2 carrots, peeled and chopped
1½ lb (750 g) tomatoes, chopped
pinch ground allspice
2 teaspoons orange peel
juice of 2 oranges
30 fl oz (940 ml) stock
5 fl oz (155 ml) plain yogurt
5 fl oz (155 ml) double (heavy) cream
salt and pepper, to taste
1 orange, peeled and chopped
1 tablespoon chopped fresh parsley, to decorate

Heat oil in a saucepan, add onion and carrots and stir-fry for 5 to 10 minutes. Mix in tomatoes, spice, orange peel and juice, pour over stock and cover tightly, then simmer gently for 30 to 45 minutes. Strain off juice and reserve. Purée pulp in a blender or food processor. Return this purée to pan, add reserved juices and reheat. Stir in yogurt, cream, salt and pepper and heat through, but do not allow to boil.

To serve, place a few pieces of chopped orange in each soup bowl, ladle on soup and sprinkle with parsley.

Tomato Ice Cream

A summer first course – keeps 6 to 8 weeks in the freezer.

Serves 4
6 large tomatoes
1 teaspoon grated orange peel
juice of 1 orange
6 fl oz (185 ml) double (heavy) cream,
whipped
1 tablespoon chopped fresh mint
salt and pepper, to taste

Purée tomatoes in a blender or food processor, then sieve to remove pips and skins. Add remaining ingredients and mix together gently. Pour into a container and freeze until firm.

Tomato & Prawn Mousse

A delicious first course or light supper dish.

Serves 4

*about 2 lb (1 kg) tomatoes or enough to
give 20 fl oz (625 ml) of tomato juice*

1 oz (30 g) powdered gelatine

4 tablespoons dry or medium sherry

*pinch cayenne pepper or a dash of Tabasco
sauce*

2 teaspoons sugar

6 oz (185 g) peeled prawns, chopped

salt and pepper, to taste

*10 fl oz (315 ml) double (heavy) cream,
whipped*

a few whole prawns, to garnish

Skin tomatoes and remove as many seeds as
possible. Purée in a food processor or blender. Melt gelatine in sherry in a small saucepan over a gentle heat, stirring constantly
until smooth – do not allow to boil. Stir in
cayenne or Tabasco and sugar and pour into
the puréed tomatoes. Leave in the fridge
until almost set, 20 to 30 minutes, then add
chopped prawns, salt and pepper and fold in
cream. Pour into a wetted mould and leave to
set in the fridge.

To serve, turn out and garnish with a few
prawns.

Hot Tomato Crumble

A great favourite with children and good with cheese dishes, bacon or ham. This is a simple dish and can be made with whatever you have in the way of tomatoes and breadcrumbs. Exact amounts are not necessary.

Serves 4
1½ lb (750 g) tomatoes
1½ oz (45 g) butter
2 spring onions, chopped
8 oz (250 g) breadcrumbs, wholemeal or white
sugar and salt and pepper, to taste

Skin tomatoes and slice thickly. Grease an ovenproof dish with some of the butter and place a layer of tomatoes with some of the spring onions and breadcrumbs. Sprinkle with sugar, salt and pepper. Repeat until ingredients are used up and dot the final layer of breadcrumbs with remaining butter. Bake for 20 to 30 minutes at 190 °C (370 °F/ Gas 5).

A cooked tomato is like a cooked oyster: ruined. (1938, Andre Simon 'The Concise Encyclopedia of Gastronomy')

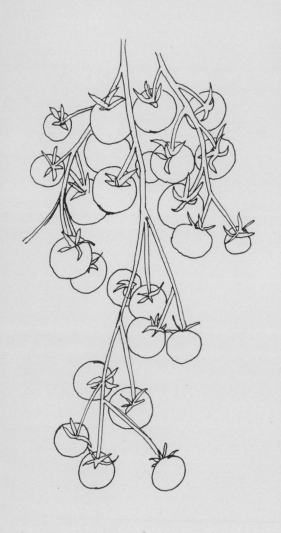

A gardeine where salet herbes do growe.

(1538, Elyot)

Tomato & Bacon Layer
A tasty supper dish and simple to prepare.

Serves 4
1 lb (500 g) tomatoes
1 tablespoon oil
1 medium onion, chopped
8 oz (250 g) bacon, roughly chopped
1 lb (500 g) breadcrumbs
1 whole egg and 2 yolks, beaten
1 teaspoon chopped fresh sage
salt and pepper, to taste
1–2 tablespoons chopped fresh parsley

Oil a 2 pint (1.25 litre) ovenproof dish liberally. Skin tomatoes and slice thickly. Heat oil in a frying pan and fry the onion until tender, then add bacon and fry for 5 minutes. In a large bowl mix together breadcrumbs, egg and yolks, then add onion and bacon mixture. Layer bacon and breadcrumb mixture with tomatoes in the prepared dish, sprinkling sage, salt and pepper on each layer. Finish with a layer of tomatoes. Bake in a moderate oven at 190 °C (375 °F/Gas 5) for 30 to 40 minutes or until set. Sprinkle with chopped parsley.

Eggs in Tomatoes

A very simple but very nice dish.

You need largish tomatoes and small eggs, 1 for each per person. Take the tops off the tomatoes, scoop out the pulp, dust with salt and pepper and break the egg into the tomato shell. Place on a buttered baking dish – I use individual soufflé ramekins – and cook in a tray of water for 5 minutes at 190 °C (375 °F/Gas 5) or until eggs are set but not hard.

The pulp can be used in a sauce or soup.

You can put everything, and the more things the better, into a salad, as into a conversation; but everything depends on the skill of mixing.

(1871, Charles Dudley Warner 'My Summer in a Garden')

Vegetables in Tomato Sauce

This quickly-made fresh tomato sauce goes well with many vegetables, such as cabbage, leeks and potatoes, as well as the more obvious courgettes (zucchini).

Exact quantities are not important for this recipe, you can use what tomatoes come to hand. As a sauce for chopped cabbage I would use:

1 oz (30 g) butter
4–5 tomatoes, skinned and roughly chopped
1 tablespoon chopped spring onions
pinch mace
salt and pepper, to taste

Melt butter in a small pan. Add remaining ingredients and gently stir-fry for 5 minutes. Pour over vegetables and serve.

Tomatoes in Sour Cream

This is a hot/cold dish particularly good if sprinkled liberally with fresh basil. Place a serving dish in oven to warm. You will need a good-sized, firm, tasty tomato per person, 1 teaspoon of butter per tomato, salt and freshly ground black pepper, 1 tablespoon sour cream and 2 teaspoons chopped fresh basil.

Halve the tomatoes, melt the butter in a frying pan and quickly cook tomatoes, sprinkling them with salt and pepper. When tender but not mushy, place on the warm serving dish and pour round the sour cream. Stir the basil into the pan juices and pour over the tomatoes. Serve at once. Hot garlic bread goes well with this dish.

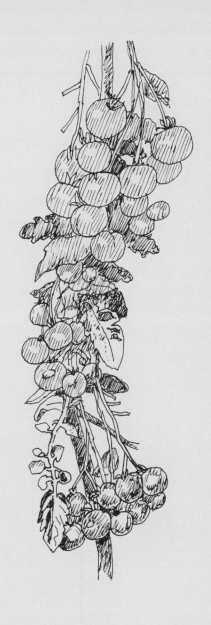

Main Course Stuffed Tomatoes

This dish is nicer if you use really large tomatoes.

Serves 4

4 large tomatoes

salt and pepper

STUFFING

1 oz (30 g) butter or 2 tablespoons oil

1 small onion, chopped

1 clove garlic, chopped

8 oz (250 g) minced meat, pork, beef or a mixture

1 slice bread, wholemeal or white, crusts removed

pinch nutmeg

Slice tops off tomatoes and reserve. Scoop out pulp and reserve in a bowl. Dust inside of tomatoes with salt and pepper, turn upside down on a wire rack and leave to drain for half an hour. Meanwhile make the stuffing.

Melt butter or oil in a frying pan, add chopped onion and cook until tender, do not allow to brown. Add garlic and minced meat and stir-fry for 5 to 6 minutes. Soak bread in reserved tomato pulp. Add meat mixture to bread mixture, nutmeg, salt and pepper and mix well.

Oil a baking sheet. Fill tomatoes about three-quarters full, replace tops and place on prepared baking sheet. Bake at 190 °C (375 °F/Gas 5) for 15 to 20 minutes, or until soft, but not shrunken or mushy.

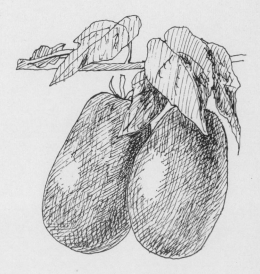

Plum Tomatoes

To make a good salad is to be a brilliant diplomatist – the problem is entirely the same in both cases. To know how much oil one must mix with one's vinegar.

(1880, Oscar Wilde 'Vera, of the Nihilists')

Iced Cherry Tomatoes

A simple but unusual starter.

   Skin some firm, ripe cherry tomatoes, chill until really cold in the fridge. Serve them with triangles of hot fried bread and accompany with a curry-flavoured mayonnaise.

Golden Tomato

According to the Spanish proverb, four persons are wanted to make a good salad: a spendthrift for oil, a miser for vinegar, a counsellor for salt and a madman to stir it all up.

(1852, Abraham Hayward 'The Art of Dining')

They are very temperate in their diet, eating a great deal of sallet and but little flesh.

(1673 Ray, Journal, Low Countries)

Tomato Custard

There are many variations of this old-fashioned dish, this one of mine includes curd cheese. Do not rush the cooking, if it is cooked quickly it will curdle and spoil.

Serves 4–5
1 lb (500 g) ripe tomatoes
5 eggs
10 fl oz (315 ml) milk
6 oz (185 g) curd cheese
*1 tablespoon chopped fresh basil or
1 teaspoon dried basil or oregano*
salt and pepper, to taste

Grease a 2 pint (1.25 litre) ovenproof dish with plenty of butter. Place tomatoes in a blender or food processor and purée until smooth, then add eggs, milk, cheese, herbs, salt and pepper. Purée again, then pour into prepared dish. Stand in a tray of water and bake at 180 °C (350 °F/Gas 4) for 45 minutes or until centre is set. Serve warm.

37

Tomato & Liver Bake

A good supper dish, slow cooking is the secret for keeping the liver moist.

Serves 4
2 oz (60 g) butter
2 onions, finely chopped
2 cloves garlic, chopped
1 bay leaf
2 teaspoons grated orange peel
juice of 1 orange
1½–2 lb (750 g–1 kg) tomatoes, sliced
1½ lb (750 g) lamb's liver in one piece
salt and pepper, to taste

Melt butter in a flameproof casserole over a low heat, add onions and garlic and stir-fry for 4 to 5 minutes, then mix in bay leaf, orange peel and juice. Add one-third of the tomatoes, lay liver on top and cover with remaining tomatoes. Sprinkle with salt and pepper, cover tightly and leave to cook on a very low heat for 45 minutes, when the liver should be cooked but still just pink in the middle. (Cook for an extra 15 to 20 minutes if you prefer your liver well done.) Take care not to overcook or the liver will become dry.

Tomato Tart

Serves 6

*8 oz (250 g) shortcrust pastry, using
6 oz (185 g) flour and 3 oz (90 g) butter
(see page 87)*

FILLING
4 tablespoons white breadcrumbs
1 lb (500 g) tomatoes, sliced
salt and pepper, to taste
3 egg yolks
4 tablespoons single (light) cream
2 tablespoons grated Parmesan cheese

Line a 9 inch (22.5 cm) tart tin with short-crust pastry. Bake blind, at 190 °C (375 °F/Gas 5) until just beginning to colour, about 15 minutes, then remove from the oven and leave aside to cool slightly.

Line pie base with breadcrumbs, arrange tomato slices in layers, sprinkling salt and pepper between each layer and bake in a hot oven, 190 °C (375 °F/Gas 5) for 10 minutes. Meanwhile, beat egg yolks and cream together. Remove pie from oven, pour cream over tomato slices and sprinkle with Parmesan cheese. Reduce oven temperature to 180 °C (375 °F/Gas 4) and cook for a further 30 to 40 minutes. Serve piping hot.

Beef & Tomatoes

A slow-cooking dish suitable for the less tender beef cuts and a good dish to freeze.

Serves 4–6

4 tablespoons oil

2 lb (1 kg) stewing beef, trimmed and cubed

1 lb (500 g) onions, chopped

2 cloves garlic, chopped

1 teaspoon allspice

2 lb (1 kg) tomatoes, skinned and roughly chopped

1 tablespoon brown sugar

2 tablespoons chopped fresh parsley, more if possible

salt and pepper, to taste

Heat oil in a heavy pan with a tight-fitting lid, add cubed meat a handful at a time and stir-fry until brown all over. Remove from pan and reserve. When all the meat is brown, add onions and garlic to pan and stir-fry for 5 to 10 minutes. Return meat to pan and add spices and tomatoes. Cover and simmer very gently for 3 to 4 hours or cook in a very slow oven, 150°–160°C (300°–375°F/Gas 2–3), until meat is very tender. Using a slotted spoon, remove meat from sauce to a serving dish and keep warm, then reduce sauce by boiling hard for 5 minutes. Add salt and pepper and pour over meat. Sprinkle with lots of parsley and serve at once.

To freeze: Pack into freezer boxes before reducing the sauce. To serve, defrost, reheat, remove meat and reduce the sauce, adding 1–2 tablespoons of tomato purée to the mixture.

Smoked Haddock on a Bed of Tomatoes

Smoked haddock goes particularly well with tomatoes.

Serves 4
1 1/2 lb (750 g) tomatoes, skinned and
sliced
2 tablespoons chopped spring onions
1 1/2 lb (750 g) smoked haddock
salt and pepper, to taste
juice of 2–3 oranges
1 1/2 oz (45 g) butter

Place a layer of tomatoes in a buttered oven-proof dish, sprinkle with half the spring onions, place the fish on top and cover with the rest of the spring onions and tomatoes. Add salt and pepper, pour over orange juice and dot with butter. Bake for 25 to 30 minutes at 180 °C (350 °F/Gas 4).

Golden, Pear-shaped Tomatoes

Tomatoes with Sugar & Orange Juice

This simple dish makes a refreshing salad.

Serves 4

1 lb (500 g) tomatoes, skinned, sliced and sprinkled with plenty of mint

MARINADE
2½ fl oz (75 ml) fresh orange juice

1 tablespoon oil

1 teaspoon vinegar

2 teaspoons made mustard, Continental type

salt and pepper, to taste

Mix all marinade ingredients together. Pour over tomatoes and leave for 15 minutes.

Tomato & Kidney Cobbler

Serves 4–5
4–5 lambs' kidneys (1 per person)
4–5 bacon slices (1 per person)
3 oz (90 g) butter
20 fl oz (625 ml) Rich Tomato Sauce (see page 47)
6 oz (185 g) self-raising flour
salt and pepper, to taste
1/2 teaspoon dried basil
milk, to mix
egg, to glaze (if desired)

Wrap each kidney in a bacon slice and secure with a toothpick. Heat 1 oz (30 g) butter in a flameproof casserole and brown bacon parcels. Pour over tomato sauce, cover with cooking foil and bake at 190 °C (375 °F/Gas 5) for 20 to 25 minutes.

Meanwhile make the scone topping. Sieve flour, salt and pepper into a mixing bowl, add herbs and rub in remaining butter until the mixture looks like fine breadcrumbs. Add enough milk, 2 to 3 tablespoons, to make a firm dough. Mix gently and form into a ball. Place on a floured working surface and roll out to 1/2 in (1 cm) thickness. Cut into small circles, triangles or squares.

Remove casserole from oven, lift off foil and place pastry shapes on top of kidney and

44

tomato mixture. Brush with egg or milk and cook for a further 20 to 30 minutes. Kidney, like liver, should not be overcooked.

Chicken with Pearl Barley & Tomatoes

Serves 4–6
2 oz (60 g) butter
one 3½–4 lb (1.75–2 kg) chicken
2 onions, finely chopped
1 carrot, peeled and chopped
*1½ lb (750 g) tomatoes, skinned and
halved*
2 oz (60 g) pearl barley
3 sticks celery, chopped
juice of 1 orange
2 teaspoons grated orange peel
salt and pepper, to taste

Melt butter in a deep, flameproof casserole. Fry chicken on all sides until nicely browned all over. Remove and set aside. Gently stir-fry onions and carrot in same fat for 4 to 5 minutes, then return chicken to pan, add tomatoes, pearl barley, celery, orange juice and peel, salt and pepper. Cover tightly and cook gently on top of stove for 1–1¼ hours or in the oven at 190 °C (375 °F/Gas 5) for the same time.

Braised Fillets of Lamb with Tomatoes

Fillets of lamb are a very tasty, economical cut but they can be fatty, so they are best gently fried to release as much of the fat as possible, then braised. One good-sized fillet will feed 2 to 3 people.

Serves 6–8
2 tablespoons cooking oil
2–3 fillets of lamb, well trimmed of fat
2 cloves garlic, chopped
1 lb (500 g) tomatoes, skinned and chopped
2 tablespoons chopped fresh marjoram
6 fl oz (185 ml) sherry, preferably dry
salt and pepper, to taste

Heat 1 tablespoon of oil gently in a frying pan, add lamb fillets and cook for 5 to 6 minutes, turning constantly. Drain off fat as it is released from meat. Remove fillets and leave to drain on absorbent kitchen paper.

Heat remaining oil in a flameproof casserole, add garlic and cook gently for 3 to 4 minutes, do not allow to brown. Add tomatoes and herbs and stir-fry for 5 to 6 minutes, then add lamb, pour over sherry and sprinkle with salt and pepper. Cover tightly and cook for 20 to 25 minutes over a low heat, do not allow to boil. Serve hot.

A Rich Tomato Sauce

6 fl oz (185 ml) olive oil
1 large onion, chopped
4 cloves garlic, chopped
2 lb (1 kg) tomatoes, skinned
1 teaspoon hot curry paste
2 tablespoons tomato purée
salt and pepper, to taste

Heat oil in a heavy pan, add onions and garlic and fry gently until soft. Add tomatoes, cover tightly and cook slowly for 30 to 40 minutes. Add curry paste and tomato purée and cook uncovered for a further 30 minutes by which time the sauce should be considerably reduced and a thick dark colour. Add salt and pepper before serving.

Vinegar Tomato Sauce

A sauce or relish to serve with fish.

4 tomatoes, skinned and finely chopped
1 teaspoon very finely chopped onion
1 tablespoon chopped fresh parsley
1 tablespoon sugar
1 tablespoon wine vinegar
2 tablespoons white wine
salt and pepper, to taste

Mix all together and serve at once.

47

Tomato Curd

This is unusual but good and can be used for cake or tart fillings. Guests will never know what it is, unless you tell them.

1 lb (500 g) tomatoes
6 oz (185 g) sugar
juice of 1 lemon
grated peel of 1 orange
2 oz (60 g) butter
2 whole eggs plus 2 yolks, beaten together
few drops pure vanilla essence

Purée tomatoes in a blender or food processor until quite smooth. Place in a heavy-bottomed pan and bring to the boil. Reduce heat and cook gently for 5 minutes. Add sugar, lemon juice and orange peel, increase heat and cook for a further 5 to 7 minutes until mixture is slightly reduced. Add butter and boil for 2 minutes. Stir in beaten eggs and cook gently until thick, but do not boil. Lastly mix in vanilla. Pot in clean, warm jars, cool and seal (see page 88). Keeps 6 to 8 weeks in a cool larder – longer in the fridge.

*Giant Fruited
Tomato*

Tomato & Candied Peel Jam

This recipe is best made with firm, not over-ripe tomatoes.

2 lb (1 kg) sugar
3 fl oz (90 ml) water
*2 lb (1 kg) tomatoes, skinned and roughly
chopped*
2 lemons, peeled and thinly sliced
4 oz (125 g) mixed peel
1/2 teaspoon allspice

Dissolve sugar in water in a heavy pan. When sugar is dissolved, boil for 2 to 3 minutes, then add tomatoes, lemons, peel and allspice and boil hard until set is reached (see page 88), 20 to 30 minutes. Remove the scum as it rises to the surface. Cool. Pot in clean, warm jars and cover (see page 88).

Lettuce – succulent, from Latin Lactuca, from Lac, milk, succulent juice.

LETTUCES

Although the lettuce is still the principal ingredient of the salad, one cannot spend the summer trying to eat up a fast bolting and running-to-seed lettuce patch: it would be simply impossible to keep up. But, having planted and nurtured the lettuces, it would be very difficult to sit back and watch them go to waste. By far the most efficient way to deal with this glut is to start cooking them! They are delicious hot, in soups or as a vegetable, and they have the advantage that, once cooked they shrink – like spinach – so you have the satisfaction of using up more in a cooked dish than you ever could have got through in a salad!

Hot Lettuce Soup

Serves 4

2 oz (60 g) butter

1 small onion, chopped

*4 lettuces, washed, trimmed of thick stalks
and finely chopped*

*20 fl oz (625 ml) chicken stock or bouillon
cube*

10 fl oz (315 ml) single (light) cream

2 tablespoons chopped cooked chicken

2 tablespoons dry sherry

salt and pepper, to taste

2 egg yolks, if desired (see method)

Melt butter in a pan, add onion and fry gently until soft. Add lettuce and stir-fry for 2 to 3 minutes, then pour in stock and simmer for 20 minutes. Stir in cream, chicken, sherry, salt and pepper and gently reheat.

If a richer, thicker soup is desired, blend two egg yolks with cream and reheat. Do not boil or soup will curdle.

Oh herbaceous treat!
'Twould tempt the dying anchorite to eat;
Back to the world he'd turn his fleeting soul,
And plunge his fingers in the salad bowl;
Serenely full, the epicure would say
'Fate cannot harm me – I have dined today.'
(1843, Sydney Smith 'Recipe for Salad')

Lettuce, like conversation, requires a good deal of oil, to avoid friction and to keep the company smooth.

(1871, Charles Dudley Warner 'My Summer in a Garden')

Chilled Lettuce Soup

Serves 4

2 tablespoons olive oil

5–6 large lettuces, washed, trimmed of thick stalks and roughly chopped

30 fl oz (940 ml) vegetable stock

6 fl oz (185 ml) double (heavy) cream

2 hard-boiled eggs, very finely chopped

pinch of mace

salt and pepper, to taste

2 tablespoons chopped fresh chives, to finish

Heat oil in a pan, add lettuces and stir-fry for 5 minutes. Stir in stock, cover and simmer for 15 to 20 minutes. Cool slightly, then purée in a blender or food processor. Pour into a bowl and place in the fridge until quite cold.

Mix in cream, then add eggs, mace, salt and pepper. Just before serving, sprinkle with chopped chives.

Batavia Endive

Webb's Wonder

Lettuce Mousse

An unusual first course for summertime. Use any variety of lettuce available for this dish. You could even use an equivalent amount of 'thinnings' left over from your salad garden.

Serves 4

2 teaspoons cooking oil

1 spring onion, very finely chopped

2 large or 3 medium lettuces, washed, trimmed and finely chopped

1 level teaspoon powdered gelatine

2 tablespoons cold water

juice of 1 orange

2 eggs, separated

6 fl oz (185 ml) plain yogurt or double (heavy) cream, or a mixture of both is best

6 oz (185 g) curd or cream cheese

pinch of mace

salt and pepper, to taste

Heat oil in a pan and quickly stir-fry spring onion and lettuce for 2 to 3 minutes. Take care lettuce doesn't lose its fresh colour. In a bowl over hot water dissolve gelatine with cold water and orange juice. Beat egg yolks together with yogurt and cream, add cheese, spice, salt and pepper to taste, mix until smooth. Add gelatine mixture, stir well and leave aside until almost setting. Beat egg whites until stiff, then fold into setting mixture with lettuce and spring onion. Chill in the fridge until completely set.

Serve chilled accompanied by a salad of sliced tomatoes.

Batavia Endive

Did I eate any lettice to supper last night that I am so sleepie?

(1614, J. Cooke)

Frisée Lettuce

Lettuce Torte

A dish to use up bolting lettuce or lettuce thinnings – or just the unwanted outside leaves.

To serve 4 you will need the equivalent of

2 good-sized lettuces. Keep the hearts or the best and most tender leaves aside, blanch the rest in boiling water. I find it easiest to do this with a large shallow pan of boiling water and, using a pair of kitchen tongs, hold each leaf submerged for a second or two until it goes dark. Do not overcook or the leaves will turn to mush. Spread them out on a wire rack to drain. As well as lettuces you need:

5 egg yolks
1 whole egg
6 fl oz (185 ml) double (heavy) cream
a little grated nutmeg
salt and pepper, to taste
2 tablespoons chopped fresh chives

Oil a 9 inch (22.5 cm) tart tin. Blanch enough leaves to double line the prepared tin – leaving enough overlap to fold over the torte – and to cover the top. Chop the hearts or tender leaves very finely. In a bowl mix together egg yolks, whole egg, cream, nutmeg, salt and pepper. Add chopped chives and lettuce hearts. Pour this mixture into prepared tin, cover carefully with blanched leaves, then cover again with foil. Place in a cool oven, 150 °C (300 °F/Gas 2), and bake for 1½ to 2 hours. Turn out and serve the torte warm.

Stuffed Lettuce: Hot

This is a quick and easy hot supper; much less complicated than it sounds. Serve with plain boiled potatoes and a green salad. The amounts of cold chicken and cheese needed will depend on the size of the lettuce.

Serves 4
1 large round lettuce

STUFFING
2 spring onions, chopped
1 tablespoon chopped fresh tarragon
4–6 oz (125–185 g) curd cheese
6–8 oz (185–250 g) cold chicken, minced
salt and pepper, to taste

TO COOK
2 tablespoons cider or water

Trim outside leaves of lettuce, cut stalk flat, so lettuce will stand upright. Gently unfold the leaves until you get to the heart, cut a deep cross in the heart and open it out. Mix all the stuffing ingredients together in a bowl. Now press the stuffing into and around the opened-out heart. Fold the outer leaves over the stuffing and press well together. Now place the lettuce stalk uppermost in a 2 pint (1.25 litre) pudding basin. Add cider or water, cover with foil, stand the basin in a saucepan of hot water, cover tightly and steam for 20 to 30 minutes until lettuce is cooked. Turn out and serve.

Webb's Wonder

A dish of Lettice and a cool Fountain can cool all my Heat.

(1678, Jeremiah Taylor)

Stuffed Lettuce: Cold

This looks very pretty, like a cauliflower instead of a lettuce, and is delicious.

Serves 4 as a main course or 6 as a starter
1 large round lettuce

STUFFING
5–6 hard-boiled eggs, mashed with a fork
2 tablespoons cream cheese
2 tablespoons mayonnaise
2 teaspoons lemon juice or wine vinegar
2 spring onions, chopped, white part only
salt and pepper, to taste
1 tablespoon milk, if desired

Trim lettuce, cut stalk flat, so lettuce will stand upright. Gently unfold the leaves until you get to the heart, cut a deep cross in the heart and open it out. Mix all the stuffing ingredients together in a bowl; if they seem too stiff add a tablespoon of milk. Place lettuce on a serving dish and fill centre with mixture, pressing outer leaves up.

Surround with tomato and olive salad.

The effect of eating too much lettuce is 'soporific'.
(1908, Beatrix Potter 'The Tale of the Flopsy Bunnies')

Let such as have sprouted be planted for Spring scallions.

(1786, Abercrombie 'Gardiner's Assistant')

Batavia Endive

Lettuce Roulade

Lettuces, like spinach, make a good roulade. Stuff with a purée of other summer vegetables and herbs – peas and mint are good.

Serves 6
8 oz (250 g) cooked lettuce, chopped very fine (see method)
1 oz (30 g) butter
1 oz (30 g) plain flour
10 fl oz (315 ml) milk
pinch mace
salt and pepper, to taste
6 eggs, separated

Lettuces are very light and you may need 2 or 3 large lettuces to give 8 oz (250 g) cooked lettuce. To cook the lettuces, trim, wash, chop and place in a pan with a tight-fitting lid, add ½ oz (15 g) butter or 1 tablespoon oil, cover and leave to cook over a gentle heat

Cos

for 3 to 4 minutes. Remove from heat, drain well, chop again.

Grease a 12 × 14 inch (30 × 35 cm) Swiss roll tin and line with non-stick paper. In a saucepan melt butter over a gentle heat, add flour and mix well. Slowly add milk, stirring all the time, until sauce is smooth; bring to the boil and cook for 1 to 2 minutes. Add mace, salt and pepper. Now beat in egg yolks one by one, then add lettuce. Beat egg whites until stiff, then fold into the lettuce mixture. Pour into prepared tin and cook for 15 minutes, at 190 °C (375 °F/Gas 5), until sides begin to shrink and middle is firm. When cooked, remove from oven, cover with a clean tea towel and leave to rest for 2 to 3 minutes, then carefully turn it over and out onto the clean tea towel, remove lining paper and either fill at once with a warm filling or leave to cool and serve cold.

*

You need the soul of a rabbit to eat lettuce as it is usually served – green leaves slightly lubricated with oil and flavoured with vinegar. A salad is only a background; it needs embroidering.

(Paul Reboux)

63

Radicchio

Lettuce as a Hot Vegetable

Small lettuces are nicest for this dish, allow 1–2 per person and leave them whole.

Serves 4
1 oz (30 g) butter
8 small lettuces, washed and trimmed
2 spring onions, chopped
1 teaspoon grated orange peel
1 tablespoon chopped fresh mint
salt and pepper, to taste

Melt butter in a pan, add lettuces, cover tightly and leave to cook for 4 to 5 minutes, shaking the pan constantly. When cooked, add the rest of the ingredients, toss well and stir-fry for 1 minute. Serve at once.

Cos

Bread Salad

A gigantic sandwich, best eaten in the garden! Traditionally the bread is spread with olive oil and garlic, then topped with lettuce, tomatoes and more garlic. The top slice, also soaked in oil and garlic, is added when you've piled on as much salad as you think you can get your mouth round.

Another version of bread salad is a tossed green salad to which you add hunks of bread to absorb the dressing. We like to make ours with homemade brown bread and butter, lots of young lettuce, mayonnaise and a spring onion.

Lettuce with Pasta

This is a lettuce sauce to use with summer pasta dishes. Any variety of lettuce may be used.

For 8 oz (250 g) uncooked pasta (serves 2–3) you will need:

1 oz (30 g) butter

1 small onion, chopped

1 large lettuce, washed and very finely chopped

2 tablespoons cooked ham, chopped

6 fl oz (185 ml) double (heavy) cream

salt and pepper, to taste

Melt butter in a pan, add onion and cook until tender, do not allow to brown. Add lettuce and stir-fry for 2 to 3 minutes, then add ham, cream, salt and pepper.

Heat thoroughly and pour over the pasta.

Lettuce with Courgettes (Zucchini)

A dish for a Chinese wok or a very large frying pan. Heat some oil in a pan, add 3 to 4 chopped spring onions, 3 to 4 thickly sliced courgettes (zucchini) and 1 head of lettuce washed, dried and chopped. Stir-fry for 2 to 3 minutes, then add 1 to 2 tablespoons dry sherry and salt and pepper, to taste. Mix well and serve at once.

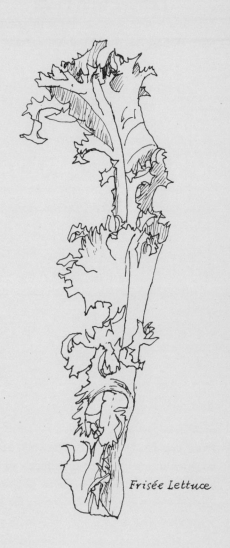

Frisée Lettuce

Much vse of lettes hurteth the eyesight.
(1562, Turner 'Herbal')

Candied Lettuce Stalks

This is an old-fashioned recipe for 'wet candied' fruits and peels. It is possible to candy lettuce stalks and use them in cakes and desserts. Use the thickest stalks from a Cos or other crisp-stalked lettuce and cut them into 2 inch (5 cm) lengths. Lettuce stalks don't need blanching in salt and are generally more tender and less stringy than angelica.

20 fl oz (625 ml) sugar syrup (see page 88)
thinly pared peel of 1 lemon
1 blade of mace
a bunch of lettuce stalks

Heat sugar syrup, lemon peel and mace in a shallow pan, place lettuce stalks in syrup and bring to a fast boil, then lower heat and simmer for 7 to 10 minutes or until stalks begin to turn transparent; do not overcook for they will continue to cook in the hot syrup. Put in a clean, warm jar and cover.

Cucumber may be treated in the same way but replace the mace with 1 inch (2.5 cm) of fresh ginger, scraped and sliced. Remember to remove the cucumber seeds; the peel may be left on.

This is reminiscent of, though not as crunchy as, that delicious Chinese dessert Chow Chow.

Radicchio

CUCUMBERS & OTHER SALAD VEGETABLES

'Those windy vegetables' – how can a glut of cucumbers be used up without the whole family complaining? But cucumbers need not necessarily be bad for the digestion – indeed nobody has yet proved conclusively that they are. Don't think of them as a small addition to a salad, as a fish decoration or as a sandwich filling for those rare occasions when a summer afternoon tea might be served. They make delicious soups, are equally good stuffed and served hot or cold, and, when gently braised, make a wonderful summer vegetable. Salad accompaniments, such as radishes, rocket and cress, also produce gluts, if on a smaller scale. But they, too, can be turned into soups or added to sauces.

Hot Cucumber Soup

This is a lovely soup even on a hot summer's day; it is very rich.

Serves 4
2 oz (60 g) butter
1 onion, finely chopped
1 large cucumber, peeled and grated
15 fl oz (470 ml) vegetable stock
10 fl oz (315 ml) milk
2 egg yolks
6 fl oz (185 ml) double (heavy) cream
1 tablespoon chopped fresh dill
salt and pepper, to taste

Melt butter in a saucepan, add onion and fry gently until tender, do not allow to brown. Add cucumber and stir-fry for 2 to 3 minutes, then add stock, bring to the boil and simmer, covered, for 10 minutes. Remove lid and cook fast for 5 minutes, then add milk and heat through. Remove from heat. In a bowl mix egg yolks with cream and stir into soup. Add dill, salt and pepper, then reheat carefully, do not boil or soup will curdle.

Cucumbers along the surface creep,
with crooked Bodies and with Bellies deep.
(1697, Dryden: Virgil's Georgics)

71

Cucumber Vinaigrette

Thinly slice the cucumber, leaving the peel on if young. Place in a colander, sprinkle with a little salt, gently toss, then cover with a plate and weight and leave to drain for 20 to 30 minutes. Remove from colander and pat dry with absorbent kitchen paper. Place in a serving dish and toss with your favourite vinaigrette recipe, to which you have added some garlic and chopped fresh herbs, such as parsley, mint or dill.

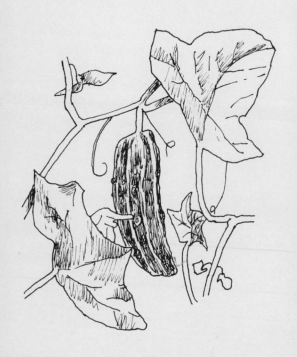

Cucumber Mousse

The secret of this dish is to line the base of the mould or ramekins with a layer of well-flavoured fish, a spoonful of curried lentils, or some chopped ham and pickled garlic.

Serves 4–6
1 level tablespoon powdered gelatine
4 tablespoons white wine
1 cucumber, peeled and grated
6 fl oz (185 ml) plain yogurt
2 tablespoons mayonnaise
1 teaspoon chopped fresh chives
1 teaspoon chopped fresh mint or dill
salt and pepper, to taste
1 egg white, stiffly beaten

In a bowl over hot water dissolve gelatine in wine, then add cucumber, yogurt, mayonnaise, herbs, salt and pepper. Mix all together and chill until almost set, then gently fold in beaten egg white and pour into a serving dish or individual ramekins lined with a layer of fish or one of the other suggested bases. Chill until completely set. Turn out to serve.

It was as dry as a stick, hard as a stone, and cold as a cucumber.

(1760, Gray)

Hot Stuffed Cucumbers

These make a special first course or a delicious main course when served with rice or new potatoes. Depending on the size of the cucumber, this should serve 4–5 as a main course.

2 cucumbers

STUFFING
10–15 fl oz (315–470 ml) dry cider
2 spring onions, chopped
2 oz (60 g) curd cheese
2 egg yolks
8 oz (250 g) cooked salmon
1 tablespoon chopped fresh dill
1 tablespoon pine nuts
1 tablespoon currants
salt and pepper, to taste

Cut cucumbers into 3 inch (7.5 cm) lengths, slice in half lengthwise and remove seeds. Place in a saucepan with cider and poach for 5 to 10 minutes, keeping them crisp. Mix all the stuffing ingredients together in a bowl, folding in the salmon carefully. Transfer warm cucumber slices to a shallow ovenproof dish and fill with stuffing. Pour round the poaching liquid, cover with foil and bake in a hot oven, at 190 °C (375 °F/Gas 5), for 10 to 15 minutes.

Cucumber & Fish Salad

This is a main course salad for a summer lunch or supper.

Serves 4

1 cucumber

1 medium onion, chopped

1 lb (500 g) cod or haddock, poached, left until cold and flaked

1 dill pickle, finely chopped

1 tablespoon capers

DRESSING

6 tablespoons olive oil

1 tablespoon wine vinegar

3 teaspoons Dijon mustard

2 tablespoons cream

2 teaspoons sugar

salt and pepper, to taste

Peel cucumber and cut it into chunks ½ inch (1 cm) square. Place in a salad bowl and add onion, fish, dill pickle and capers, mixing gently together. Place dressing ingredients into a screw-topped jar and shake well, then pour over cucumber mixture, mix and leave to marinate for 30 minutes before serving.

The salad is the glory of every French dinner and the disgrace of most in England.

(1846 Ford, Gatherings from Spain)

Cucumber & Chicken

This is an exquisite summer dish and can be eaten hot or cold.

Serves 4
4 chicken breasts, very fresh
2 tablespoons olive oil
1 clove garlic, crushed
1/2 large or 1 small cucumber, peeled,
seeds removed and grated
2 tablespoons chopped fresh mint
6 fl oz (185 ml) plain yogurt
2 tablespoons double (heavy) cream
salt and pepper, to taste

Trim chicken breasts of all fat. Gently heat oil in a heavy frying pan and very slowly fry chicken breasts, 4–5 minutes each side. Add garlic, cucumber and mint. Toss chicken well in this mixture. Mix together yogurt and cream in a bowl, then pour over chicken and cucumber. Add salt and pepper, heat gently through and serve at once, or leave until cold.

77

Hot Cucumber & Dill

Serves 4

2 cucumbers

POACHING LIQUOR
15 fl oz (470 ml) water
2 teaspoons wine vinegar
2 teaspoons sugar
salt, to taste

SAUCE
2 tablespoons double (heavy) cream (if desired – improves taste and helps stabilize yogurt)
6–8 fl oz (185–250 ml) plain yogurt
2 egg yolks, beaten
1 tablespoon chopped fresh dill
pepper, to taste

Peel the cucumbers, cut in half lengthwise, remove seeds and cut into 2½ in (5 cm) lengths. Place all poaching ingredients in a saucepan, add cucumber and poach for 8 to 10 minutes until just tender. Drain well, place in a deep serving dish and keep warm while you make the sauce.

Place all sauce ingredients in a heavy-bottomed saucepan and cook gently over a low heat, stirring all the time until sauce begins to thicken. Do not boil, as this sauce curdles very easily, especially if you omit the cream.

Note: yogurt sauces can be stabilized by

adding a little cornflour – 1 small teaspoon
mixed with a little cold milk would be enough
for the above sauce – but it does change the
texture of the finished dish.

Hot Cucumber as a Vegetable

One cucumber serves 3 to 4 people. If young,
do not peel, slice into 1 inch (2.5 cm) rings
and poach for 5 to 7 minutes in ½ oz (15 g)
butter, 2 tablespoons dry sherry and 1 teaspoon soy sauce. Add salt and pepper just
before cooking time is up, but as soy sauce is
salty, be careful with the seasoning.

Cucumber Sauce

A favourite with fish or chicken.

Peel, seed and very finely chop half a cucumber. Place in a saucepan with ½ oz (15 g) butter, cover and leave to cook over a gentle heat for a few minutes. Add 1 teaspoon of the white part of a spring onion, finely chopped, 1 tablespoon dill, 2 to 3 teaspoons wine vinegar, 4–6 fl oz (125–185 ml) double (heavy) cream and salt and pepper to taste. Heat through, stir, then pour into a sauce boat and serve.

A cucumber should be well sliced, and dressed with pepper and vinegar, and then thrown out as good for nothing.

(1773, Dr. Samuel Johnson 'Boswell's Tour to the Hebrides')

Cucumber Relish

This sweet relish is very popular with children and looks pretty in its jar: a clear, pale green.

Makes 4–5 lb (2–2¹/₂ kg)

4 cucumbers, minced or very finely chopped

2 large onions, minced or chopped

1 small red pepper, minced or chopped

2–3 teaspoons salt

8 oz (250 g) sugar

20 fl oz (625 ml) wine vinegar

1 tablespoon cornflour

2 tablespoons water

1 teaspoon dry curry powder

1 tablespoon mustard seed

Place chopped vegetables in a bowl, sprinkle with salt and leave overnight. Strain. Place vegetables, sugar and vinegar in a pan and bring gently to the boil; boil for ³/₄ to 1 hour. Blend cornflour and water together in a bowl, add spices, then add to the mixture in the pan. Cook for a further 20 to 30 minutes. Pour into clean, warm jars and cover (see page 88).

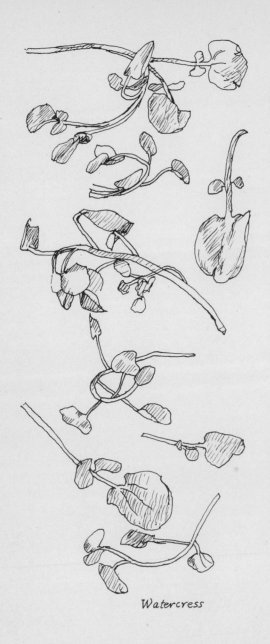

Watercress

To make sownde Teeth. Take Watercresse and rubbe the same with wine, and heerwith washe your mouth often times.

(1599, AM tr Gabelhouer's Bk Physicke)

Watercress Sauce

I always feel that this sauce should be densely green to look at and equally dense to taste. So often watercress sauce is a thick white sauce with a few green leaves and a rather floury taste.

I use 1 good bunch of watercress, chopped very finely, sweat it for 1 to 2 minutes in ½ oz (15 g) butter, add 2 tablespoons white wine and reduce by a third. Pour in 6–8 fl oz (185–250 ml) double (heavy) cream to which you have added 1 to 2 beaten egg yolks, reheat gently, add salt and pepper to taste and serve at once. The amount of cream varies according to the size of the bunch of watercress; the important thing is to keep the sauce rich and creamy.

Watercress Dressing

An accompaniment for fish or chicken, good
also on baked potatoes.

2 bunches watercress
1 tablespoon orange juice
1/2 teaspoon grated orange peel
6 fl oz (185 ml) Greek-style yogurt
2 tablespoons double (heavy) cream
salt and freshly ground black pepper

Wash watercress and dry gently in a teatowel.
Remove coarse stems and divide remainder
into 2 portions. Chop one portion very finely.
Mix together orange juice and peel, yogurt,
cream, salt and pepper in a salad bowl, add
chopped watercress and mix well. Add remaining watercress and toss gently.

Cress Sauce

Chop cress like parsley, one small box (a
good handful) will give enough taste and
colour to 6–8 fl oz (185–250 ml) of stock or
pan juices. Adding one teaspoon chopped,
preserved ginger, salt and pepper to taste and
a couple of tablespoons of white wine or one
of sherry will help the flavour. Serve with
escalopes of pork or chicken.

Water Cresse being boiled in wine ... is verie
good against the scurvie.

(1597, Gerarde, Herbal)

Rocket

Rocket

A strong, hot-tasting brassica, used a lot in
the Middle East. It is often thought of as
similar to dandelion, not in flavour, but in
use. I add it to mixed salads, or make a bed of
rocket and lettuce to put cold stuffed vegetables on.

We will have a bunch of redishes, and salt, to
taste our wine.

(1598, B. Jonson)

A Radish & Ginger Dish

This is good as a relish to accompany fish or cold meats, but I like it best on its own with wholemeal bread and butter as a summer starter.

As a first course you need 8–12 radishes per person. Trim, wash and slice thinly. For 4 people mix together the ingredients below, pour over radishes and leave to marinate for 2–3 hours.

MARINADE
4 tablespoons olive oil
2 tablespoons wine vinegar
1 teaspoon Dijon mustard
1 tablespoon chopped preserved ginger
1 tablespoon ginger syrup
1 teaspoon grated fresh ginger root
1 tablespoon chopped spring onion
salt and pepper, to taste

Some Physitians commend the eating of radishes before meate.

(1620, Venner)

BASICS

Plain Shortcrust Pastry
Suitable for savoury and sweet tarts.

8 oz (250 g) flour
1/2 teaspoon salt
4 oz (125 g) butter or margarine, hard and cold
3–4 tablespoons ice-cold water

Sift flour and salt into a mixing bowl. Cut fat into flour using two knives or a pastry cutter and mix briefly in a food processor or rub in with fingertips. When mixture looks like breadcrumbs, add water and draw together; the mixture should be very stiff. Knead together against the sides of the bowl, then wrap in plastic wrap and leave in a cool place or the bottom of the fridge for 30 minutes or until you wish to use it. If left for several hours or overnight, the pastry should be brought to room temperature for 2 to 3 hours before use.

Sugar Syrup

Yields approx. 20 fl oz (625 ml)
6 oz (185 g) sugar
15 fl oz (470 ml) water

Put the sugar and water together in a heavy-bottomed saucepan. Heat gently until sugar has dissolved, then boil fast for 3 to 5 minutes. The syrup should have a creamy consistency and coat the back of a spoon. Leave to cool.

To Test Jam for Set

Remove saucepan or preserving pan from heat and put a little jam or jelly on to a cold plate. Leave to cool, then tilt the plate slightly. The jam is setting if it begins to wrinkle at this point.

If using a sugar thermometer, 'set' is reached at 110 °C/220 °F.

To Pot Jam, Curd or Preserves

Potting must be done correctly to keep food from developing bacteria.

Make sure that the jars are completely sterile, warm and dry. Remove any foam that may have formed on the surface of the jam and pot carefully and quickly. Fill jars to the brim, cover with wax circles, then seal with self-sealing lids. Label and store in a cool, dark place or the fridge, as directed.

Storing & Freezing

Salad vegetables are some of the fastest to produce a glut and almost impossible to freeze fresh. Tomatoes are best turned into purées, sauces and chutneys. The rest of the salad glut should ideally be used up as it comes along – a lettuce purée would freeze for a few days or even for a week or two but the subtle and delicate flavour is easily lost. Cucumbers, like tomatoes and lettuces, do not freeze. Radishes, rocket and cresses are best used fresh.

INDEX

Stuffed Cucumbers, Hot   74
Stuffed Lettuce: Cold   60
Stuffed Lettuce: Hot   58
Stuffed Tomatoes, Main Course   34
Sugar Syrup   88

To Pot Jam, Curd or Preserves   88
To Test Jam for Set   88
Tomato & Bacon Layer   29
Tomato & Candied Peel Jam   49
Tomato & Kidney Cobbler   44
Tomato & Liver Bake   38
Tomato & Orange Soup   23
Tomato & Prawn Mousse   25
Tomato & Yogurt Soup   22
Tomato Crumble, Hot   27
Tomato Curd   48
Tomato Custard   37
Tomato Ice Cream   24
Tomato Sauce, A Rich   47
Tomato Tart   39
Tomatoes   11, 12, 13, 21
Tomatoes in Sour Cream   32
Tomatoes, Beef &   40
Tomatoes, Stuffed, Main Course   34
Tomatoes with Sugar & Orange Juice   43

Vegetables in Tomato Sauce   31
Vinegar Tomato Sauce   47

Watercress Dressing   84
Watercress Sauce   83

If your point be rest, take Lettuce and cowslip wine.

(1733, Alexander Pope)